HUMAN RIGHTS & LIBERTY

by

Charlie Ogden

©2017
Book Life
King's Lynn
Norfolk PE30 4LS

ISBN: 978-1-78637-118-8

Written by:
Charlie Ogden

Edited by:
Grace Jones

Designed by:
Drue Rintoul

CONTENTS

Words in **bold** can be found in the glossary on page 31.

WHAT ARE HUMAN RIGHTS?

There are certain things that people can do because the law allows them to, for example drive cars, watch television and travel around the world. However, many people argue that there are certain things that people should always be allowed to do simply because they are human. These things are known as human rights and they help people to live with **freedom**, equality, **justice** and peace.

Not everyone agrees on what is and what isn't a human right. However, there are a few rights that most people agree that everyone has simply because they are human. They are:

- The right to liberty
- The right to life
- The right to equality
- The right to a fair trial
- The right to freedom of speech
- The right to freedom of religion

Don't worry if you don't understand what these rights mean at the moment, we will talk about all of them later on!

SOME PEOPLE ARGUE THAT THERE ARE OVER 30 BASIC HUMAN RIGHTS.

Here are three Buddhists practising their right to freedom of religion.

4

WHAT IS A RIGHT?

A right is something that someone has the **authority** or permission to perform. A person might have permission to do something because the law says they can, which is called a **legal** right. For example, adults have the legal right to **vote**. Similarly, a person might have permission to do something because it is the fair thing to do, which is called a **moral** right. For example, you have the moral right to tell a teacher about a bully.

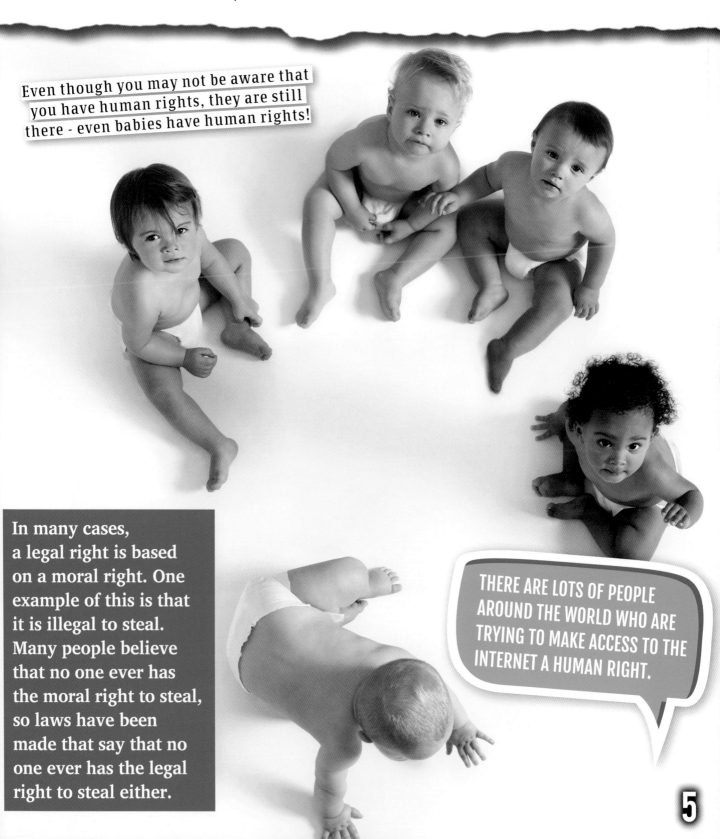

Even though you may not be aware that you have human rights, they are still there - even babies have human rights!

In many cases, a legal right is based on a moral right. One example of this is that it is illegal to steal. Many people believe that no one ever has the moral right to steal, so laws have been made that say that no one ever has the legal right to steal either.

THERE ARE LOTS OF PEOPLE AROUND THE WORLD WHO ARE TRYING TO MAKE ACCESS TO THE INTERNET A HUMAN RIGHT.

THE RIGHT TO EQUALITY

Every person has the right to live in a **society** that promotes the equality of all people. Such a society will view everyone as equally important, give everyone the same rights and allow everyone the same opportunities. This makes the right to equality very important as it states that all of the other human rights must be equally applied to everyone.

IN SAUDI ARABIA, WOMEN ARE OFTEN NOT SEEN AS EQUAL TO MEN. EVERY WOMAN IN SAUDI ARABIA MUST HAVE A MALE **GUARDIAN**, WHO OFTEN MAKES MANY OF THEIR DECISIONS FOR THEM.

Saudi Arabia

The right to equality has been one of the most difficult rights to protect because some cultures around the world do not consider everyone to be equal. Often women are not treated equally to men, sometimes not being allowed to get an education or have a job. People who do not have their right to equality protected by their **government** can be made to feel rejected and powerless.

THE RIGHT TO FREEDOM OF RELIGION

Nowadays, people from many different religions and faiths often live together very happily. In communities like this, people are used to **respecting** a person's right to practise whatever religion they like. However, there are places in the world where the right to freedom of religion isn't always respected and people are forced to stop practising their faith.

A person's right to freedom of religion can be a very important right to respect. One of the reasons for this is because a person's **identity** can often be very closely linked to their religion, as people often make their faith a significant part of their lives. In these circumstances, if a person's right to freedom of religion isn't respected, it can feel like an attack on them personally. Because of this, it is important to always respect a person's right to freedom of religion.

THE MOST RELIGIOUSLY DIVERSE COUNTRY IN THE WORLD IS SINGAPORE, WHICH HAS LARGE POPULATIONS OF BUDDHISTS, CHRISTIANS, MUSLIMS, TAOISTS AND HINDUS.

Singapore

These men are Hindus, which means that they follow the religion of Hinduism.

THE RIGHT TO A FAIR TRIAL

The right to a fair trial is an important right for governments to respect as it protects people from being unfairly punished. When someone is accused of committing a crime in a country that respects the right to a fair trial, they will get an opportunity to defend themselves.

They can put forward evidence to prove that they didn't commit the crime in **court**. A **judge** and a **jury** will look at this evidence and might agree that the person never committed the crime, meaning that they won't be punished.

This is a judge. Judges sometimes have a small hammer, known as a gavel, which they hit against a block to get the court's attention.

In places where the right to a fair trial isn't respected, people are often punished as soon as they are accused of a crime. They aren't given a chance to defend themselves. This can lead to a lot of people being punished for crimes that they haven't committed.

THE RIGHT TO FREEDOM OF SPEECH

The right to freedom of speech means that everyone should be able to voice their opinions in public. This is not limited to just speaking in public, but also includes writing your opinions in a book or even on the internet. Freedom of speech protects a person's right to discuss their own opinions without being punished or **censored**.

The right to freedom of speech is important because it helps to create change in a society by protecting a person's ability to criticise their country or government. When people speak out against their country and demand change, they can make other people in their country want to fight for change as well. This can lead to a lot of improvements being made.

Martin Luther King Jr. made his famous 'I Have a Dream' speech in 1963 and changed the way that people thought about equality in America. He could not have done this without his right to the freedom of speech.

THERE ARE MANY COUNTRIES IN THE WORLD WHERE PEOPLE DON'T HAVE THE RIGHT TO FREEDOM OF SPEECH, SUCH AS NORTH KOREA AND MYANMAR.

North Korea

Myanmar

WHY ARE HUMAN RIGHTS IMPORTANT?

Human rights are important because they protect everyone – no matter who you are or where in the world you live, you are protected by human rights. Human rights are able to protect people because they are universal, internationally guaranteed and able to limit the amount of power a government has over their **citizens**. These things can make it more difficult for a government to use the people in their country for their own gain.

UNIVERSAL

If something is universal it means that it applies to everyone and that it is true everywhere. For example, it is a universal truth that dogs can't breathe underwater. Human rights are universal because everyone on the planet has human rights.

If something is universal it means that it applies to every single person, no matter where they live in the world.

INTERNATIONAL GUARANTEE

The fact that human rights are universal has helped to make them internationally guaranteed. Some of the most important organisations in the world, such as Human Rights Watch and governments from some of the world's most powerful countries, have agreed to protect the human rights of every person on the planet. While human rights are designed to protect people, human rights themselves also need to be protected so that they aren't taken away from people. It is often difficult for a person to protect their own human rights, which is why many organisations have dedicated themselves to protecting the rights of people all over the world. Unfortunately, the governments in some countries are so controlling that these organisations find it very difficult to protect the human rights of their citizens.

MANY COUNTRIES IN AFRICA HAVE STRICT GOVERNMENTS THAT MAKE IT DIFFICULT FOR ORGANISATIONS TO PROTECT THE HUMAN RIGHTS OF THEIR CITIZENS, SUCH AS SOUTH SUDAN AND THE DEMOCRATIC REPUBLIC OF CONGO.

South Sudan

South Sudan

DR Congo

DR Congo

INFLUENCE ON GOVERNMENTS

Human rights can often have a lot of influence on governments - especially the right to life. The human right to life means that nobody, not even the government, can try to end a person's life. It also means that everyone has a right to food, water and shelter, as these are the basic things that people need in order to live. Most people are able to provide these things for themselves.

However, in cases where people aren't able to provide these things for themselves, their government has a **duty** to help and to try to provide these things for them. Governments are influenced by human rights because they have a duty to make sure that the human rights of all of the people in their country are being respected and protected.

EVERY YEAR, THE UK GOVERNMENT PROVIDES EMERGENCY HOUSING FOR THOUSANDS OF PEOPLE WHO FIND THEMSELVES HOMELESS. IN DOING SO, THE UK GOVERNMENT IS RESPECTING THEIR RIGHT TO LIFE.

Human rights also stop governments from having too much power over the public. They prevent governments from stopping people from having children, not giving people a fair trial in court and using people as slaves, among other things. As human rights are universal, these things shouldn't ever happen to anyone. However, some governments have been known to ignore the human rights of their citizens.

Nowadays, the international guarantee that comes with human rights has helped to stop these things from happening as often. If a government was found to be using the people in its country as slaves today, other governments and organisations around the world would try to stop them. Governments are not forced by law to respect human rights, rather the international guarantee that human rights will always be protected makes most governments think twice about going against them.

WHAT IS LIBERTY?

One of the most important human rights is the right to liberty, because it gives people freedom. This right states that all people can choose how they live their lives. It means that people have the freedom to choose what they wear, what they eat, where they live and where they work. Unfortunately, governments have been known to not always respect every person's right to liberty and people have been forced by their governments to live in certain places and work in certain jobs.

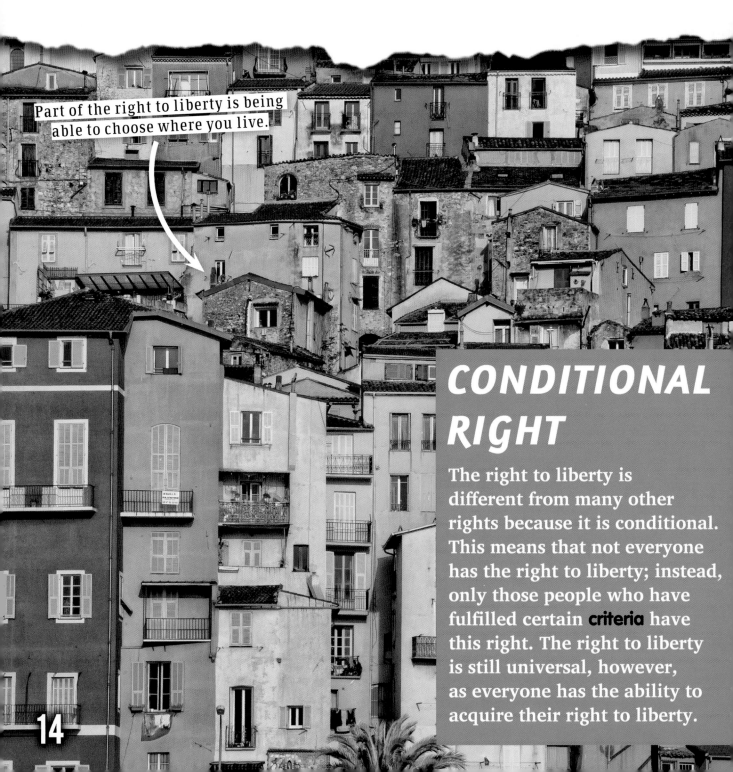

Part of the right to liberty is being able to choose where you live.

CONDITIONAL RIGHT

The right to liberty is different from many other rights because it is conditional. This means that not everyone has the right to liberty; instead, only those people who have fulfilled certain **criteria** have this right. The right to liberty is still universal, however, as everyone has the ability to acquire their right to liberty.

During the first few years of every person's life they do not have the right to liberty, even though they have many other rights. Children do not usually have the right to choose where they live or what they eat; a child's parents or guardians decide this. In most countries, people don't have the right to liberty until they reach a specific age.

TODAY, OVER 10 MILLION PEOPLE AROUND THE WORLD ARE IN PRISON. OVER 2 MILLION OF THESE PRISONERS ARE IN THE UNITED STATES OF AMERICA, MAKING IT THE COUNTRY WITH THE HIGHEST NUMBER OF PRISONERS IN THE WORLD.

Another example of people who don't have the right to liberty are prisoners, who lose their right to liberty when they break the law. Once someone breaks the law they can lose their right to liberty and no longer be able to choose where they live. Putting a person in prison can be seen as the government taking away their liberty as a form of punishment.

WHY IS LIBERTY IMPORTANT?

Liberty is one of our most basic **necessities** as human beings. For thousands of years, early humans had liberty and never had to worry about it being taken away. They became very used to having to make decisions about where they were going to live, what they were going to eat and what job they were going to do. After all of these years of having to make tough decisions about our lives, many people believe that humans have developed a natural desire to choose certain things about their lives.

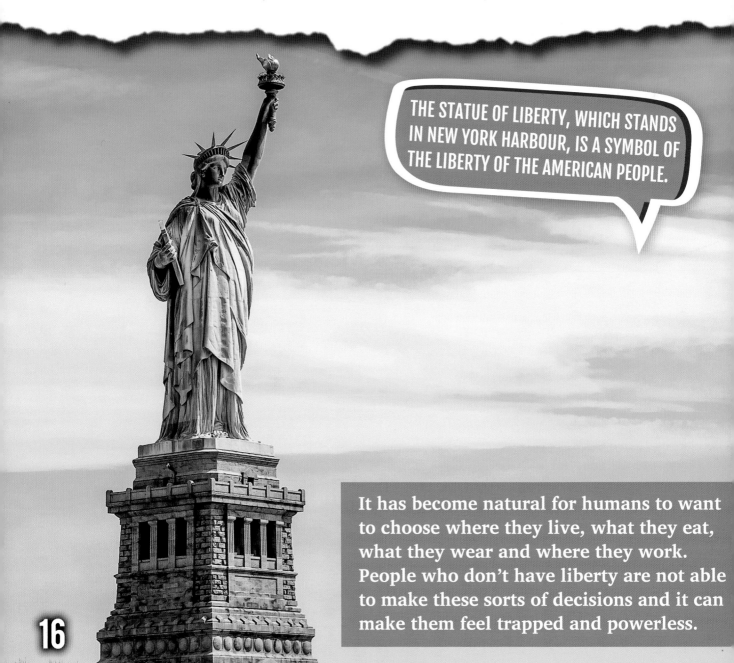

THE STATUE OF LIBERTY, WHICH STANDS IN NEW YORK HARBOUR, IS A SYMBOL OF THE LIBERTY OF THE AMERICAN PEOPLE.

It has become natural for humans to want to choose where they live, what they eat, what they wear and where they work. People who don't have liberty are not able to make these sorts of decisions and it can make them feel trapped and powerless.

HAPPINESS

Liberty is one of the most important human rights because it allows people to be happy. A lot of people are happy with their lives because they feel that they have achieved something. This may be because they have been able to buy the house of their dreams or because they have finally got the job that they always wanted. For people to be able to feel this sense of achievement, they need to have liberty. If they didn't have liberty and were forced to live in certain houses or work in certain jobs, then they wouldn't feel as proud about their lives. Being proud of what you have achieved in life is one of the main sources of happiness for people, but this is taken away if a person doesn't have liberty.

THE WORLD HAPPINESS REPORT HAS SHOWN THAT THE HAPPIEST COUNTRIES IN THE WORLD, WHICH ARE DENMARK, SWITZERLAND AND ICELAND, ARE ALSO THE COUNTRIES WHERE CITIZENS HAVE THE GREATEST AMOUNT OF LIBERTY.

This is Copenhagen, the capital city of Denmark.

MAKING BETTER SOCIETIES

Many people have argued that the importance of liberty is mostly down to the positive effect that it has on societies. Societies where people don't have the right to choose what job they do can often become very boring. This is because people don't have the opportunity to start new and exciting businesses that can bring life and colour to their community, such as new restaurants, art galleries and activity centres. In contrast to this, societies where people can choose what job they do often have streets lined with interesting restaurants and shops because people have been able to start any business that they want!

This street in London shows how just how bright and exciting streets can be!

People who have the freedom to choose where they live will usually choose to live in the nicest places possible. These places might have less crime, better schools and more green, open spaces. However, problems can occur when somewhere becomes **overpopulated**, as this can make it difficult to provide enough food, water and electricity for all of the people who live there.

To stop everyone in a society from wanting to live in one place, other places in that area have to improve. This gives people more choice of decent places to live, which makes it less likely that individual places will become overpopulated. From this, some people argue that if a society allows people the freedom to choose where they live, more places in that society will become nice places to live.

KOWLOON WALLED CITY IN HONG KONG WAS ONE OF THE MOST OVERPOPULATED PLACES IN THE WORLD BEFORE IT WAS DESTROYED IN 1994 TO MAKE ROOM FOR A NEW PARK. AT ONE POINT, OVER 33,000 PEOPLE WERE LIVING IN KOWLOON WALLED CITY, WHICH ONLY COVERED AN AREA OF 0.01 SQUARE MILES.

Kowloon Walled City, Hong Kong.

HUMAN RIGHTS AND LIBERTY IN HISTORY

ATHENS

Liberty has been seen as a human right since the time of the Ancient Greeks. One city in particular, Athens, is noted for giving its citizens more liberty than any other country did for hundreds of years after. While Athens is now the capital city of Greece, 2,500 years ago it was an **independent** city that acted much like a country does today.

This is the Parthenon, an extremely old temple in Athens that would have been very important during ancient times.

ATHENS WAS NAMED AFTER ATHENA, THE GREEK GODDESS OF WISDOM AND JUSTICE.

Athens was certainly ahead of its time, but it was not perfect. While rich men were mostly allowed to do what they pleased, not everyone else in the city was as lucky. Many wealthy people in Athens used lots of slaves so that they had more free time to work on the government. These slaves were unpaid, forced to work and couldn't choose anything about their lives. Basically, they had no liberty.

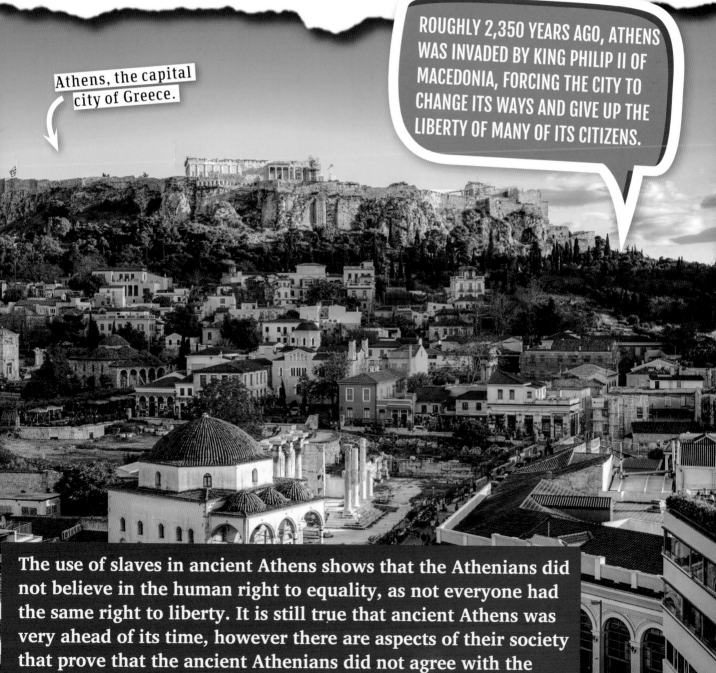

Athens, the capital city of Greece.

ROUGHLY 2,350 YEARS AGO, ATHENS WAS INVADED BY KING PHILIP II OF MACEDONIA, FORCING THE CITY TO CHANGE ITS WAYS AND GIVE UP THE LIBERTY OF MANY OF ITS CITIZENS.

The use of slaves in ancient Athens shows that the Athenians did not believe in the human right to equality, as not everyone had the same right to liberty. It is still true that ancient Athens was very ahead of its time, however there are aspects of their society that prove that the ancient Athenians did not agree with the modern view of human rights.

LIBERTY IN THE U.S.A.

Since its formation on the 4th of July, 1776, the United States of America has been one of the best countries at giving its citizens liberty. The Declaration of Independence is a document that was written by the people who made the U.S.A. an independent country and it outlines certain rules and rights for the American citizens. One line in this document has become famous as one of the first **official** statements made about human rights.

The Declaration of Independence was written to give America, which at the time only had thirteen states, independence from Great Britain.

The Declaration of Independence.

"We hold these truths to be self-evident, that all men are created equal, that they are endowed by their Creator with certain unalienable rights, that among these are life, liberty and the pursuit of happiness."

Many of the things that we associate with human rights today, such as equality, a right to life and a right to liberty, can be seen in this quote from the Declaration of Independence, which was written nearly 250 years ago.

WORLD WAR TWO

Human rights did not fully grow into the idea that we know today until after World War Two. This war, which lasted from 1939 to 1945 and involved many of the most powerful countries in the world at the time, brought about so many **atrocities** that people began to think that basic human rights should be put in place in order to protect people.

One event in particular started the idea of human rights: the Holocaust. The Holocaust is the name we give to the killing of **Jews** that occurred during World War Two at the hands of the German Nazis. During the Holocaust, over 6 millions Jews were killed, many of whom were children. This, along with a great number of other atrocities that occurred during the war, made people believe that human rights were extremely important.

THE NUMBER OF JEWS IN THE WORLD STILL HASN'T RETURNED TO THE AMOUNT THAT THERE WAS BEFORE THE HOLOCAUST.

St Paul's Cathedral in London during World War Two. It is surrounded by fires caused by bombs.

Many major cities were bombed during World War Two, killing lots of innocent people.

23

An organisation made up of governments from all around the world was established immediately after World War Two. It was made to promote cooperation between countries and to prevent a war like World War Two from ever happening again. The organisation is known as the United Nations, often just called the UN for short, and it is still very important today.

The UN composed the Universal Declaration of Human Rights in 1948. This declaration was signed by 48 different countries and includes all of the rights talked about at the beginning of this book, as well as many others. Many consider this declaration to be part of international law, meaning that all of the countries who signed it have an **obligation** to respect and protect the human rights of everyone on the planet.

THE UNITED NATIONS WAS MADE TO REPLACE A PREVIOUS ORGANISATION CALLED THE LEAGUE OF NATIONS.

The United Nations created the Universal Declaration of Human Rights in Paris on the 10th of December, 1948.

After the Universal Declaration of Human Rights was signed, many countries improved their position on human rights. However, it took some countries a lot longer than others.

NELSON MANDELA WAS THE FIRST BLACK PRESIDENT OF SOUTH AFRICA. HE SPENT 27 YEARS IN PRISON FOR TRYING TO PROMOTE EQUALITY IN HIS COUNTRY.

This is the flag of South Africa.

One country that took many years to begin respecting human rights was South Africa. South Africa did not sign the Universal Declaration of Human Rights in 1948 because its apartheid system did not respect human rights. Among other things, the apartheid system forced black people in South Africa to live in certain areas so that they were separated from white people. This shows that the South African government at the time did not respect their citizens' right to liberty. However, in 1994 South Africa got a new government, led by Nelson Mandela, and it finally removed the apartheid system and began to respect the human rights of its people.

HUMAN RIGHTS AND LIBERTY TODAY

Today, lots of countries around the world have laws to protect the human rights of their citizens. The UK government passed the Human Rights Act in 1998, which explained how the UK government should respect the human rights of the UK public. It included many more rights than just the ones mentioned in this book, such as the right to **privacy**, the right to freedom of thought and the right to peaceful **protests**.

However, this law goes further than just saying that the UK government must respect the rights of its citizens. Under the Human Rights Act, people in the UK are allowed to take the government to court if they believe that the government hasn't respected their human rights. This helps to protect the rights of the UK public even more.

CANADA AND SAN MARINO ARE CONSIDERED BY MANY PEOPLE TO HAVE SOME OF THE BEST HUMAN RIGHTS LAWS IN THE WORLD.

San Marino

Canada

San Marino

While the state of human rights in the world is much better today than it has ever been in history, there is still a long way to go. This becomes very clear when we think about how many people alive today are slaves. While no one is certain about the exact number, most people agree that there are more than 25 million slaves in the world today. Many of these people were promised paid work in foreign countries, but when they arrived in these countries they were forced to work for nothing. Slaves today often have to work far away from their homes and families and they have little hope of escaping the slavery that they have been forced into.

THERE ARE ROUGHLY 14 MILLION PEOPLE TRAPPED IN SLAVERY IN INDIA TODAY, WHICH IS MORE THAN ANY OTHER COUNTRY IN THE WORLD.

India

MUNSHIGHAT मुंशी घाट

Varanasi, India is one of the oldest cities in the world.

HUMAN RIGHTS
CASE STUDIES

MALALA YOUSAFZAI

In Pakistan, the human right to equality is not respected and many women do not have the same right to education as men. One girl in particular, Malala Yousafzai, understood how wrong this was and, in 2009, began speaking out against the lack of education for girls in her country. For years Malala continued to talk about the poor state of human rights in Pakistan and the fact that women find it very difficult to get an education. However, in 2012 Malala was shot on her way to school by someone who did not agree with her beliefs. She was only 15 years old at the time.

IN 2014, MALALA YOUSAFZAI WAS AWARDED THE NOBEL PEACE PRIZE, MAKING HER THE YOUNGEST PERSON TO EVER RECEIVE THE AWARD.

Luckily, Malala survived the attack and has since moved to the UK where she has been able to continue her education. Malala is now seen by many as a symbol of equality and human rights.

Malala Yousafzai.

This is the Pakistan Monument in Islamabad, the capital city of Pakistan.

AUNG SAN SUU KYI

Aung San Suu Kyi is a Burmese **politician** who has made great changes to the state of human rights around the world. Aung was arrested in 1989 because she was organising peaceful protests and criticising the Burmese government for, among other things, not respecting the human rights of its citizens. Aung was put under house arrest, meaning that she wasn't allowed to leave her house, for nearly 15 years. Aung didn't have her right to freedom of speech, her right to a fair trial or her right to liberty respected by the Burmese government.

Shwedagon Pagoda in Yangon, Myanmar.

AUNG IS NOT ALLOWED TO BE THE PRESIDENT OF MYANMAR BECAUSE SHE MARRIED SOMEONE FROM ANOTHER COUNTRY – AN ENGLISH HISTORIAN NAMED MICHAEL ARIS.

Since getting out of prison Aung has made a lot of changes to the government in Myanmar (Burma), which in 2015 had its first **democratic election**. She has supported human rights and equality all over the world and is considered one of the most important people ever in the fight for liberty.

Aung San Suu Kyi

ACTIVITY

What do you think is the most important human right?
Can you explain why?

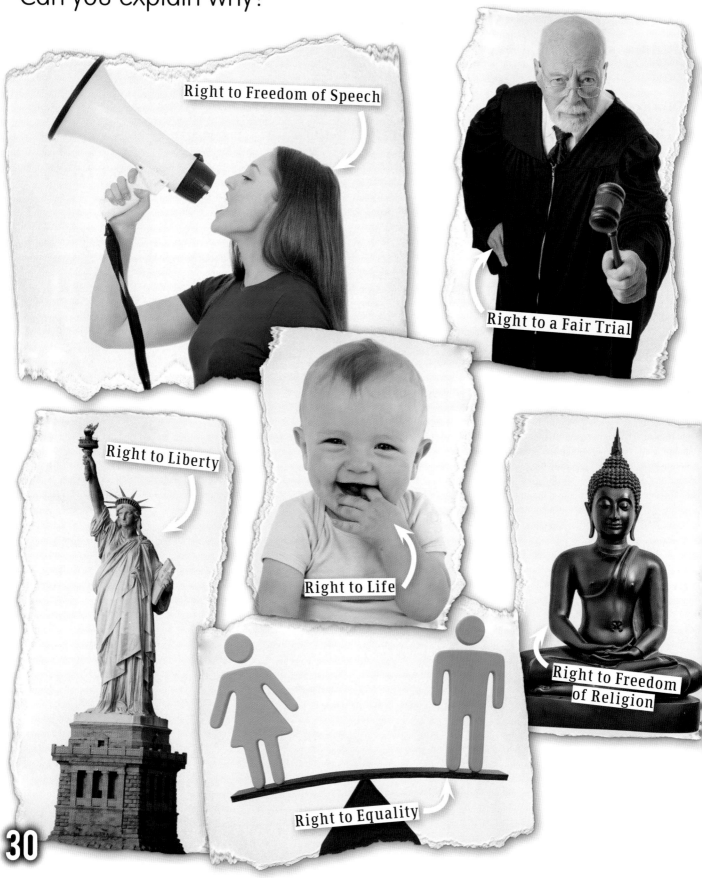

Right to Freedom of Speech

Right to a Fair Trial

Right to Liberty

Right to Life

Right to Freedom of Religion

Right to Equality

GLOSSARY

atrocities	extremely cruel acts
authority	the power to give orders or make decisions
censored	to have an opinion suppressed or hidden by an authority
citizens	legally recognised members of a country
court	a group of people brought together to settle criminal disputes
criteria	standards that need to be met
democratic election	where everyone in a country gets an equal vote
duty	a moral or legal responsibility
freedom	the power to act, speak and think as one wants to
government	the group of people with the authority to run a country
guardian	a person who protects or owns something
identity	a person's view of who they are
independent	free from outside control or authority
Jews	people who follow the religion of Judaism
judge	the person appointed to decide cases in court
jury	a group of ordinary people who go to court in order to fairly decide whether someone has committed a crime
justice	that which is right and fair
legal	relating to the law
moral	relating to what's right and wrong
necessities	things that are required
obligation	something that a person is morally or legally required to do
official	relating to an authority, such as a government
overpopulated	somewhere where people live in excessively large numbers
politician	a person who is professionally involved in the government and politics
privacy	to not be observed or disturbed by other people
protests	actions expressing disapproval of or objection to something
respecting	considering the feelings, wishes and rights of other people
society	lots of people living together in an ordered community
vote	to make a decision about who you want in your government

INDEX